Little People, BIG DREAMS®
MARCUS RASHFORD

Written by
Maria Isabel Sánchez Vegara

Illustrated by
Guilherme Karsten

Frances Lincoln
Children's Books

In a humble district of Manchester, England, lived a boy who spent all day practising with his football. His name was Marcus, and though he didn't have much, he felt rich. He had his family's love and his neighbours' affection.

His mother worked from dawn to dusk to bring food to the table. She even skipped meals to make sure her children had enough to eat.

Even so, the family had to rely on free
school meals and the help of food charities.

Marcus was five when he started playing as a goalkeeper for a local football club. As they polished their skills on the playing field, the girls and boys learnt not only to be good players on the pitch, but even better people off it.

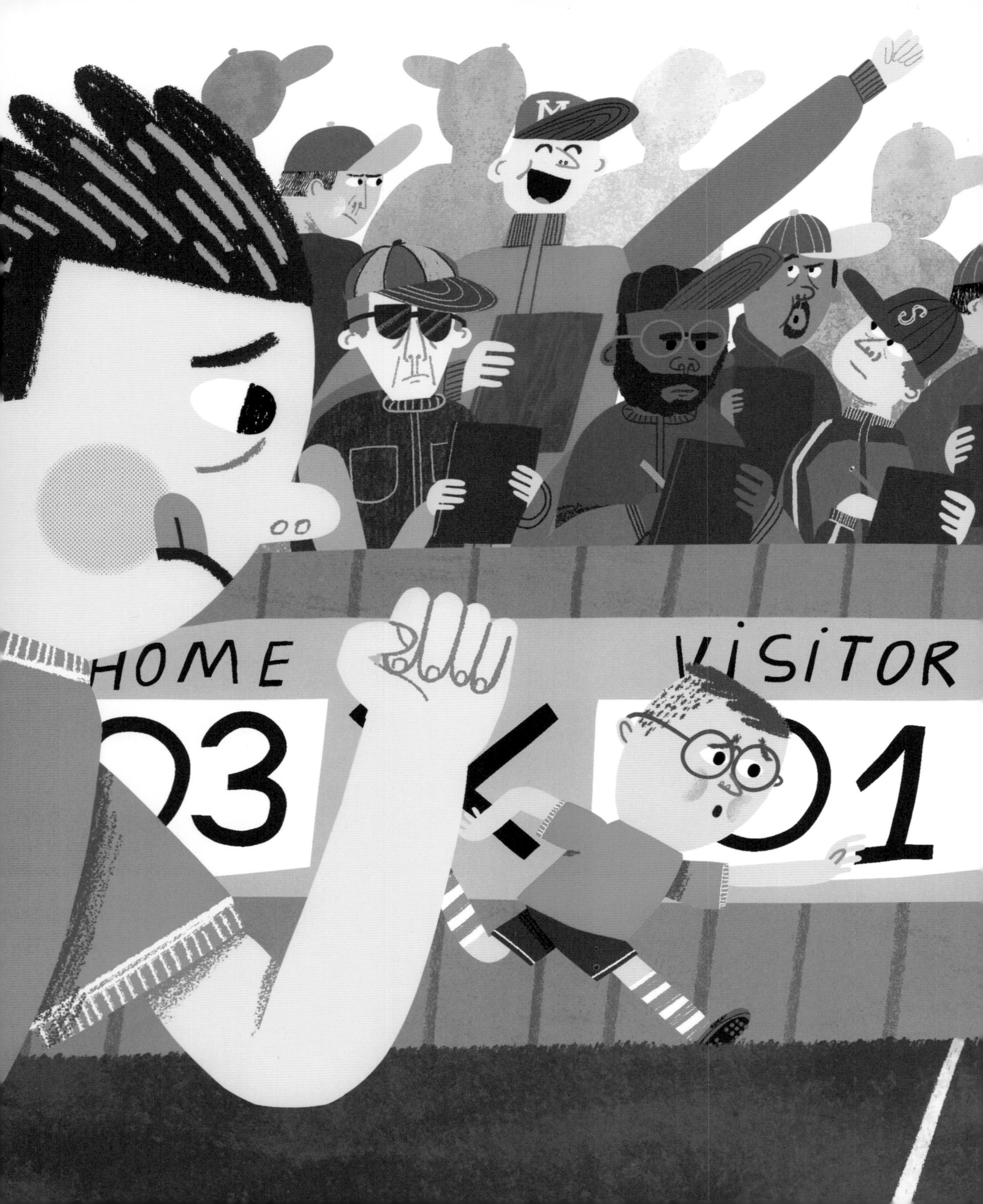
HOME
03
VISITOR
01

Marcus went from defending the goal to being the best at attacking it. The day he helped his team win a tournament, 15 scouts were watching. Soon, he joined the academy at Manchester United – one of the top teams in the world!

For eleven years, Marcus worked hard to become a great forward. Every time he played, he felt he was doing it not only for himself, but for his family, friends and everyone in the neighbourhood who had shared his dream.

When he was given a place on the first team, Marcus knew this was his chance to show those who believed in him that he deserved their trust. He had to sit on the bench for three long months... but in his debut game, he scored two goals!

Three months later, he pulled on the national team shirt of England, ready to give his best. That day, he became the youngest player to score for his country in his first match. He was only 18 years old.

One day, a global pandemic hit the country. Even schools had to close. Children who relied on free school meals were given food vouchers instead. But Marcus realised many families in his hometown still struggled to feed their children.

Marcus worked with a food charity to make sure that no child would go to bed hungry – not just in Manchester, but across the country. He also wrote a letter to the government asking them to keep helping families during the holidays.

News on paper

MARCUS RASHFORD member of the British Empire.

The next day, even the Queen was talking about his letter!
It forced politicians to help those in need and it turned
Marcus into a role model for the next generation. He had
sparked a sense of solidarity all around the country.

Marcus felt prouder than ever when he represented England as part of the Euro 2020 squad.

The team knelt at the beginning of every game, sending a message of unity, equality and justice.

Sadly, Marcus and two others missed their penalties in the final match shoot-out. A few noisy and angry people wrote terrible, racist things about them.

But everyone else in the country felt proud of their players. People came out to support Marcus and stand up to the bullies.

Marcus
thank you
for everything

And, as long as there is a cause worth fighting for, little Marcus will be there to give a helping hand. Because stars only become true heroes when they inspire others to stand together for what is right.

MARCUS RASHFORD

(Born 1997)

c. 2012   2014

Marcus Rashford was born on 31st October 1997 in Manchester, England.
He loved football as a kid and joined Fletcher Moss Rangers at the age
of five. His mother, Melanie, worked hard to provide for her children, but
there were times when they relied on food charities, and Marcus ate free
meals provided by his school. He was scouted by Manchester United and
joined its youth academy. In February 2016, Marcus made his Premier
League debut and after exceptional performances for Manchester United,
he represented England at the age of 18. In March 2020, as the COVID-19
pandemic took hold, the world shut down – football games were stopped
and schools closed. Knowing the changes would leave people in hardship,
Marcus partnered with a charity to help feed families in his hometown and

2020

2021

across the UK. He called on the government to end childhood food poverty, and a day later, it was announced that children would receive free meals during school holidays. He was awarded an MBE in October 2020 for his service to the country. Marcus represented England in the 2020 European Championship, held in 2021. When he missed a penalty during the final match against Italy, he was subjected to racist abuse, but people came together to condemn racism and support Marcus and his teammates. Later that year, he became the youngest recipient of an honorary doctorate from the University of Manchester for his charitable work and his sporting achievements. With his determination to better the lives of kids with stories like his own, Marcus is an inspiration on and off the pitch.

Want to find out more about **Marcus Rashford?**

Have a read of this great book:

Ultimate Football Heroes: Rashford by Matt and Tom Oldfield

Brimming with creative inspiration, how-to projects, and useful information to enrich your everyday life, quarto.com is a favourite destination for those pursuing their interests and passions.

Text © 2022 Maria Isabel Sánchez Vegara. Illustrations © 2022 Guilherme Karsten.

Original idea of the series by María Isabel Sánchez Vegara, published by Alba Editorial, S.L.U.

"Little People, BIG DREAMS" and "Pequeña & Grande" are trademarks of
Alba Editorial S.L.U. and/or Beautifool Couple S.L.

First published in the UK in 2022 by Frances Lincoln Children's Books, an imprint of The Quarto Group.

The Old Brewery, 6 Blundell Street, London N7 9BH, United Kingdom.

T (0)20 7700 6700 **www.Quarto.com**

A catalogue record for this book is available from the British Library.

ISBN 978-0-7112-7097-8

eBook ISBN 978-0-7112-7100-5

Set in Futura BT.

Published by Katie Cotton and Peter Marley • Designed by Lyli Feng

Edited by Lucy Menzies and Claire Saunders • Production by Nikki Ingram

Editorial Assistance from Rachel Robinson

Manufactured in Guangdong, China CC082022

3 5 7 9 8 6 4

Photographic acknowledgements (pages 28-29, from left to right):1. Wales U16 v England U16 - Sky Sports Victory Shield Under 16 International - Genquip Stadium, Port Talbot, Wales - 1/11/12. © Action Images/Steven Patson/REUTERS via Alamy Stock Photo. 2. MANCHESTER, ENGLAND - SEPTEMBER 13: Marcus Rashford of Manchester United in action during the Barclays Under-18 Premier League match between Manchester United U18s and Stoke City U18s at the Aon Training Complex on September 13 2014 in Manchester, England. © John Peters via Getty Images. 3. Marcus Rashford MBE and mum Melanie visiting FareShare Greater Manchester at New Smithfield Market. © Mark Waugh via Alamy Stock Photo. 4. OCTOBER 07: Marcus Rashford of Manchester United poses after receiving an honorary doctorate from the University of Manchester at Old Trafford on October 07, 2021 in Manchester, England. © Tom Purslow via Getty Images

Collect the *Little People,* **BIG DREAMS®** series:

FRIDA KAHLO	**COCO CHANEL**	**MAYA ANGELOU**	**AMELIA EARHART** 	**AGATHA CHRISTIE**	**MARIE CURIE**	**ROSA PARKS**	**AUDREY HEPBURN**
EMMELINE PANKHURST	**ELLA FITZGERALD**	**ADA LOVELACE**	**JANE AUSTEN** 	**GEORGIA O'KEEFFE** 	**HARRIET TUBMAN**	**ANNE FRANK**	**MOTHER TERESA**
JOSEPHINE BAKER	**L. M. MONTGOMERY**	**JANE GOODALL**	**SIMONE DE BEAUVOIR** 	**MUHAMMAD ALI**	**STEPHEN HAWKING**	**MARIA MONTESSORI**	**VIVIENNE WESTWOOD**
MAHATMA GANDHI	**DAVID BOWIE**	**WILMA RUDOLPH**	**DOLLY PARTON**	**BRUCE LEE**	**RUDOLF NUREYEV** 	**ZAHA HADID**	**MARY SHELLEY**
MARTIN LUTHER KING JR.	**DAVID ATTENBOROUGH**	**ASTRID LINDGREN**	**EVONNE GOOLAGONG**	**BOB DYLAN** 	**ALAN TURING** 	**BILLIE JEAN KING** 	**GRETA THUNBERG**
JESSE OWENS	**JEAN-MICHEL BASQUIAT**	**ARETHA FRANKLIN**	**CORAZON AQUINO**	**PELÉ** 	**ERNEST SHACKLETON**	**STEVE JOBS**	**AYRTON SENNA** 
LOUISE BOURGEOIS	**ELTON JOHN**	**JOHN LENNON**	**PRINCE**	**CHARLES DARWIN**	**CAPTAIN TOM MOORE** 	**HANS CHRISTIAN ANDERSEN**	**STEVIE WONDER**

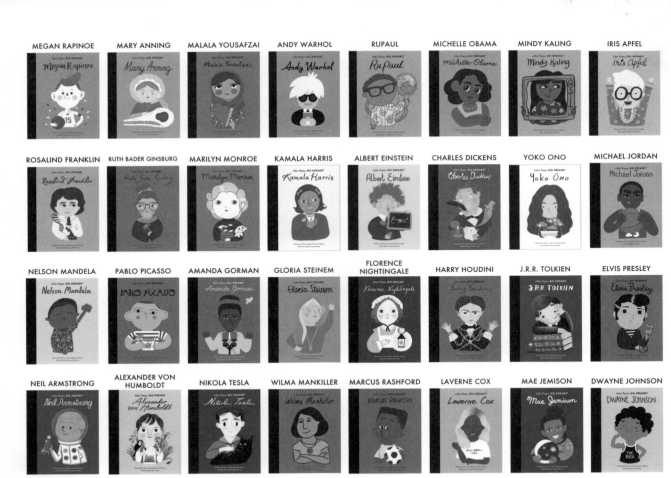

MEGAN RAPINOE	MARY ANNING	MALALA YOUSAFZAI	ANDY WARHOL	RUPAUL	MICHELLE OBAMA	MINDY KALING	IRIS APFEL

ROSALIND FRANKLIN	RUTH BADER GINSBURG	MARILYN MONROE	KAMALA HARRIS	ALBERT EINSTEIN	CHARLES DICKENS	YOKO ONO	MICHAEL JORDAN

NELSON MANDELA	PABLO PICASSO	AMANDA GORMAN	GLORIA STEINEM	FLORENCE NIGHTINGALE	HARRY HOUDINI	J.R.R. TOLKIEN	ELVIS PRESLEY

NEIL ARMSTRONG	ALEXANDER VON HUMBOLDT	NIKOLA TESLA	WILMA MANKILLER	MARCUS RASHFORD	LAVERNE COX	MAE JEMISON	DWAYNE JOHNSON

HELEN KELLER	ANNA PAVLOVA	QUEEN ELIZABETH	TERRY FOX

ACTIVITY BOOKS

STICKER ACTIVITY BOOK   COLOURING BOOK   LITTLE ME, BIG DREAMS JOURNAL

Discover more about the series at www.littlepeoplebigdreams.com

Marcus you inspira us!
Luke
we are so prou of YO
CHAM-PION
MARC-US
we love YOU
hope
LOVE
YOU ARE
ENGLAND
OUR HER
LOVE MARCUS
thank you, marcus
HE RO!
it's TRUE
Love
Marcus
thank you for everything You do!
marcus is the BEST
I ♥ M
THAN